Mini Artist
Drawing

Paul Calver

WINDMILL
BOOKS
New York

Published in 2015 by Windmill Books, An Imprint of Rosen Publishing
29 East 21st Street, New York, NY 10010

Editor for Windmill: Joshua Shadowens

Photo Credits: Illustrations by Fiona Gowen; Images on pages 4 and 5 © fotolia.com.

Library of Congress Cataloging-in-Publication Data

Calver, Paul.
 Drawing / by Paul Calver.
     pages cm. — (Mini artist)
 Includes index.
 ISBN 978-1-4777-9115-8 (library binding) — ISBN 978-1-4777-9116-5 (paperback) —
 ISBN 978-1-4777-9117-2 (6-pack)
 1. Drawing—Technique—Juvenile literature I. Title.
 NC655.C35 2015
 741.2—dc23
                                2014001243

Manufactured in the United States of America

CPSIA Compliance Information: Batch #WS14WM: For Further Information contact Windmill Books, New York, New York at 1-866-478-0556

Mini Artist **Drawing**

Contents

Getting Started

The projects in this book use lots of art materials that you will already have at home. Any missing materials can be found in an art supply store.

pencil

ruler

sharpener

eraser

felt-tip pens

colored pencils

crayons

chalks

Handy Hint

Most of the greatest artists in the world keep sketch books. Try practicing in a sketch book before you start each project.

Here is a gallery of all the paper you will need to complete all the drawing projects.

Happy Faces

To create these happy faces, you will need a piece of white paper, a pencil and an eraser.

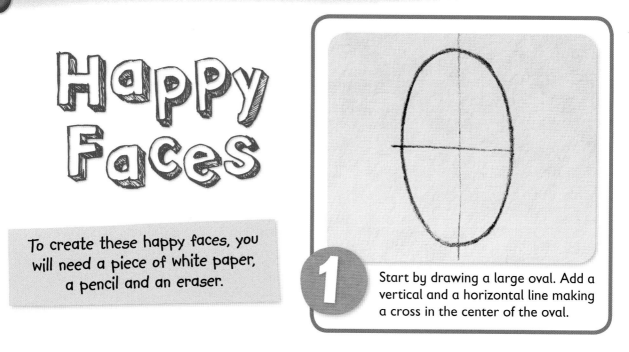

1 Start by drawing a large oval. Add a vertical and a horizontal line making a cross in the center of the oval.

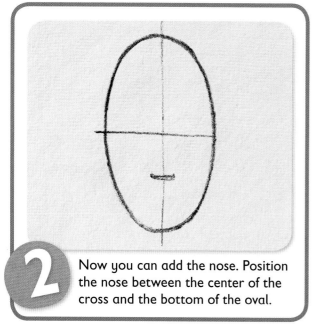

2 Now you can add the nose. Position the nose between the center of the cross and the bottom of the oval.

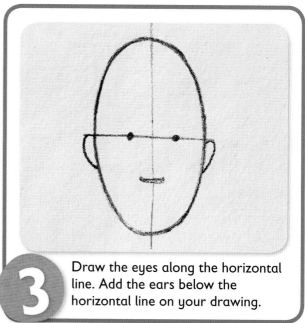

3 Draw the eyes along the horizontal line. Add the ears below the horizontal line on your drawing.

4 Now add the mouth to your picture. Draw the mouth half-way between the nose and the bottom of the oval.

5 To finish your face drawing, you can add a hairstyle. Try drawing long hair that is tucked behind the ears.

6 Try using different face shapes and hairstyles. Erase the cross when you are happy with the drawing.

8

Squiggly Fish

To make this crazy picture, you need some paper, some colored pencils and a black felt-tip pen.

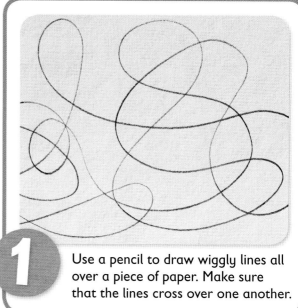

1 Use a pencil to draw wiggly lines all over a piece of paper. Make sure that the lines cross over one another.

2 Pick an orange pencil to color some of the fish shapes. Choose shapes that are not next to each other.

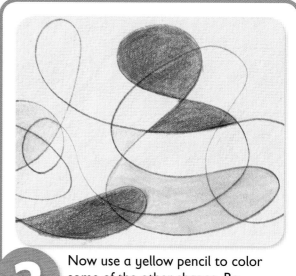

3 Now use a yellow pencil to color some of the other shapes. Be careful not to color over the lines.

4 Use a blue pencil to color all of the other shapes. The blue area will be the water that the fish swim in.

5 Use a black felt-tip pen to go over the outlines of the orange and yellow shapes. These are the fish.

6 Finish your squiggly fish drawing by using a black felt-tip pen to draw an eye onto each fish.

In the Country

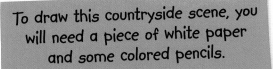

To draw this countryside scene, you will need a piece of white paper and some colored pencils.

1 Start your picture by drawing three green wavy lines across your paper. These lines will become the hills.

2 Add some trees to your drawing. The trees in the **background** must be smaller than the ones in front.

3 Use a gray pencil to draw a road across the hills. Add some markings along the middle of your road.

4 Now add some bushes to your drawing. Color the bushes a darker shade of green than the trees.

5 Add a small pink and purple house on the top of the hill. Now shade the grass in a light green color.

6 Finish your drawing by adding a sun and clouds in the sky, and some flowers on the grass.

Sailing Away

To make this boating picture, you will need some white paper and some colored pencils.

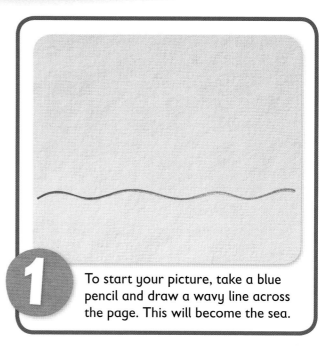

1 To start your picture, take a blue pencil and draw a wavy line across the page. This will become the sea.

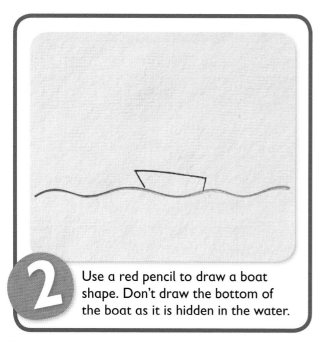

2 Use a red pencil to draw a boat shape. Don't draw the bottom of the boat as it is hidden in the water.

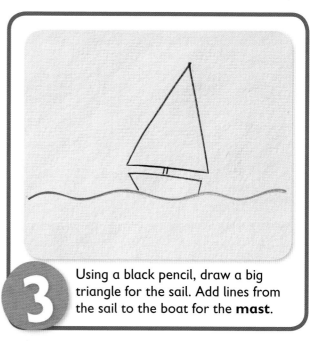

3 Using a black pencil, draw a big triangle for the sail. Add lines from the sail to the boat for the **mast**.

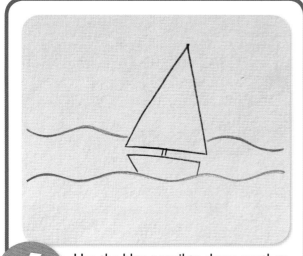

4 Use the blue pencil to draw another wavy line above the first. This line should stop when it reaches the sail.

5 You can add a yellow sun in the sky. Use a black pencil to draw some shapes for birds flying over the sea.

6 Finish by shading in the sea, boat and the sun. You could add some fish swimming in the sea.

14

Pretty Butterfly

This butterfly is easy to create. All you will need is some blue paper and some crayons.

1 Use a purple crayon to draw a long oval for the body, a circle for the head and two lines for the **antennae**.

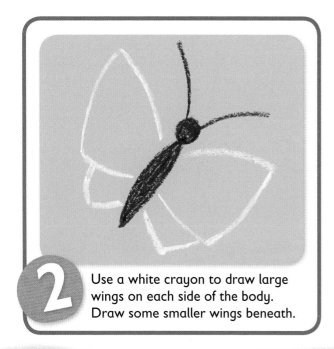

2 Use a white crayon to draw large wings on each side of the body. Draw some smaller wings beneath.

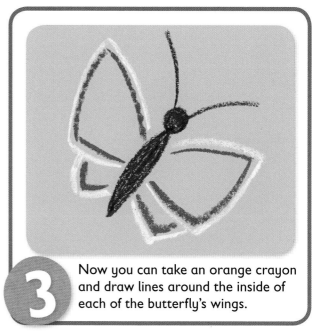

3 Now you can take an orange crayon and draw lines around the inside of each of the butterfly's wings.

4 Use the same orange crayon to draw some dots on the wings. Draw small yellow circles around each dot.

5 Now you can use the white crayon to draw bigger circles around each of the dots on the butterfly's wings.

6 To finish your picture, draw some pretty flowers for the butterfly to flutter around.

Blasting Off!

To make this outer space picture, you will need plain black paper and some colored chalk.

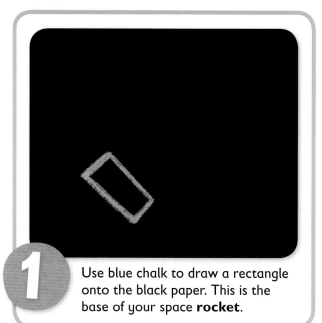

1 Use blue chalk to draw a rectangle onto the black paper. This is the base of your space **rocket**.

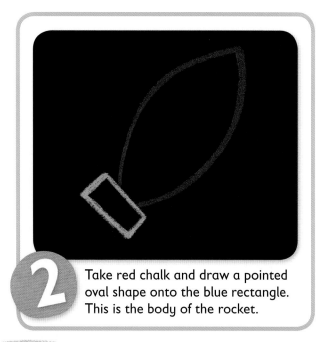

2 Take red chalk and draw a pointed oval shape onto the blue rectangle. This is the body of the rocket.

3 Now you can use orange chalk to draw small triangles under the blue rectangle. These will be the jets.

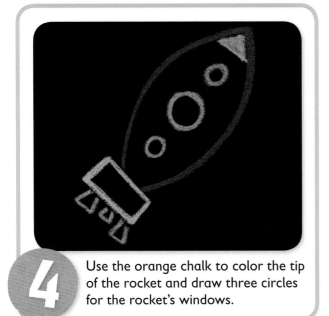

4 Use the orange chalk to color the tip of the rocket and draw three circles for the rocket's windows.

5 To put the finishing touches on your space rocket, use your red chalk to add two wings to the body.

6 Decorate the space background with lots of stars and planets. You can also add some other spacecraft.

Simple Buildings

To make these simple buildings, you will need graph paper, some felt-tip pens and a ruler.

1 Start your drawing by using a green felt-tip pen and a ruler to draw a horizontal line for the ground.

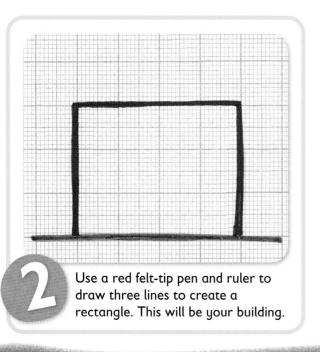

2 Use a red felt-tip pen and ruler to draw three lines to create a rectangle. This will be your building.

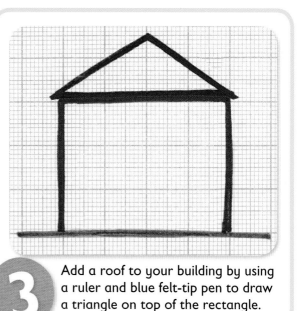

3 Add a roof to your building by using a ruler and blue felt-tip pen to draw a triangle on top of the rectangle.

4 Use a bright yellow felt-tip pen to draw the front door of the house. The door should be a tall rectangle.

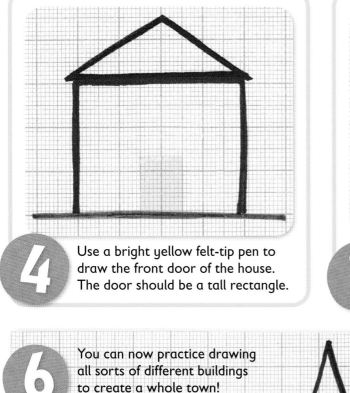

5 Add windows by drawing four squares. Draw a cross through each square to show the window panes.

6 You can now practice drawing all sorts of different buildings to create a whole town!

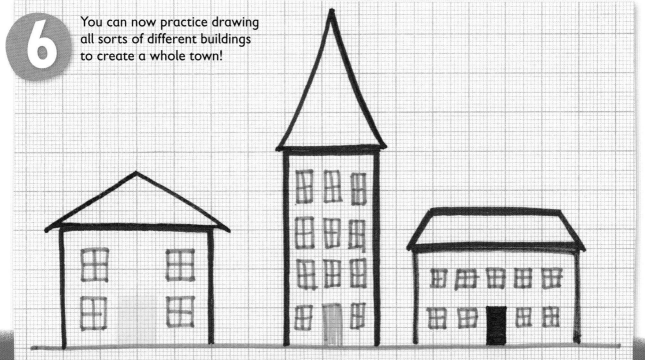

Fancy Flowers

To create these flowers you will need some colored pencils and a large piece of green paper.

1 Start your drawing by using an orange pencil to draw a small circle. This will be the center of the flower.

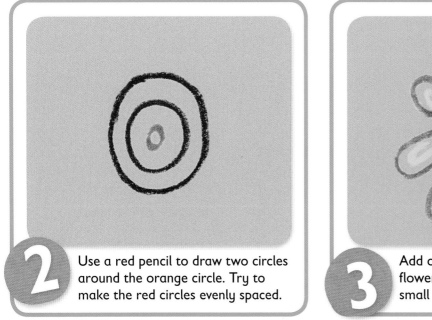

2 Use a red pencil to draw two circles around the orange circle. Try to make the red circles evenly spaced.

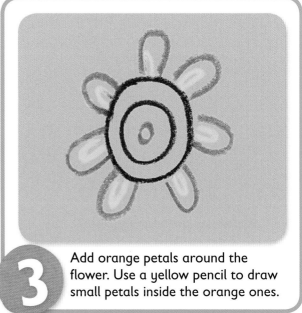

3 Add orange petals around the flower. Use a yellow pencil to draw small petals inside the orange ones.

4 Now add the stem of the flower. Use a green pencil to draw a straight line beneath the flower.

5 Using your green pencil, add leaves to the stem. Try to make each pair of leaves the same size and shape.

6 To finish the picture, add a line for the ground and then practice adding flowers in different styles.

Funny Robots

These funny **robots** are easy to draw. You will need some colored pencils and white paper.

1 Start the picture by drawing a rectangle with an orange pencil. This rectangle is the robot's head.

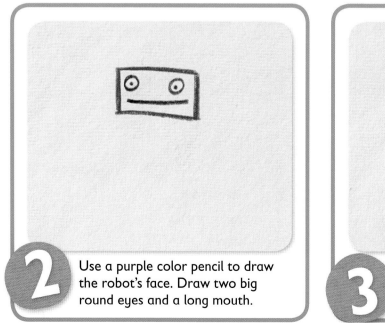

2 Use a purple color pencil to draw the robot's face. Draw two big round eyes and a long mouth.

3 Draw an orange four-sided shape for the robot's body. Add the antenna to the top of the head.

4 Use the orange pencil to draw the neck, arms and legs. Add small lines across to make a ladder pattern.

5 Take the orange pencil and add crescent shapes and semi-circles to make the robot's hands and feet.

6 Try making more robots using different shapes and colors. Now color all the robots in.

Glossary

antennae (an-TEH-nee) Thin, rodlike organs used to feel things, located on the head of certain animals.

background (BAK-grownd) The part of a picture or scene toward the back.

mast (MAST) A long pole that rises from the deck of a ship and holds the sails and ropes.

robots (ROH-bots) Machines made to do jobs that often people do.

rocket (RAH-ket) A machine with a powerful engine that pushes it into the air.

Index

Further Reading

Eason, Sarah. *Drawing Baby Animals*. Learn to Draw. New York: Gareth Stevens, 2014.

Gray, Peter. *How to Draw Butterflies and Other Insects*. How to Draw Animals. New York: PowerKids Press, 2014.

Websites

For web resources related to the subject of this book, go to: www.windmillbooks.com/weblinks and select this book's title.